The Tiny Book of Golf Jokes

The Tiny Book of Golf Jokes

Robert McCune

Illustrated by
Peter Townsend

HarperCollins*Publishers*

HarperCollins*Publishers*
77–85 Fulham Palace Road,
Hammersmith, London W6 8JB

www.**fire**and**water**.com

This paperback edition 2000
3 5 7 9 8 6 4 2

Previously published in Great Britain
by Angus & Robertson (UK) 1998

Copyright © Mary Coleman 1988

The Author asserts the moral right to
be identified as the author of this work

ISBN 0 00 710496 0

Set in Stone Sans by Rowland Phototypesetting Ltd,
Bury St Edmunds, Suffolk
Printed and bound in Great Britain by Scotprint

'I'd move heaven and earth to be able to break 100 on this course,' sighed the veteran.

'Try heaven,' advised the caddie. 'You've already moved most of the earth.'

'I see a Russian says he has invented a game which closely resembles golf.'

'Oh yes, my husband's been playing that for years.'

Jeff was in bad form when he came home.

'What's the matter dear?' asked his wife.

'Dr Hyde says I can't play golf,' growled her husband.

'Oh, dear,' gasped the anxious wife. 'Did he see you at the hospital?'

'No, playing golf.'

What do you do when your opponent claims to have found his ball in the rough and you know he's a liar because his ball is in your pocket?

A golfing friend is one who can remember every shot you missed but doesn't remind you.

'Hey, George, did you hear the awful news about John?'

The two golfers were talking over a drink in the club bar.

'No what happened to him?'

'Well he had a great round on Wednesday – under seventy I heard – anyway he finished early and drove home, and found his wife in bed with another man! No questions asked . . . he just shot 'em both! Isn't it terrible?'

'Could have been worse,' George commented.

'How?'

'If he'd finished early on Tuesday, he would have shot me!'

'What's your golf score?' the country club interviewer asked the prospective new member.

'Well, not so good,' replied the golfer. 'It's 69.

'Hey, that's not bad. In fact, it's very good.'

'Glad you think so. I'm hoping to do even better on the next hole,' the golfer confided.

'Just got a brand new set of clubs for my husband.'

'Oh what a good trade!'

'Now remember,' said the husband as he played for the first time with his wife, 'I don't like to talk when I'm playing.'

'You don't need to,' retorted his wife, 'just listen.'

Roger and Charlie emerged from the clubhouse to tee off at the first, but Roger looked distracted.

'Anything the matter, mate?' Charlie asked.

'Oh, it's just that I can't stand the club pro,' Roger replied. 'He's just been trying to correct my stance.'

'He's only trying to help your game,' Charlie soothed.

'Yeah, but I was using the urinal at the time.'

'It was golf that drove me to drink,' W. C. Fields once admitted, 'and you know, I don't know how to thank it.'

'Frankly,' said W. C. Fields, 'I'd rather play a nine-hole course as it uses up less valuable drinking time.'

Man blames fate for other accidents but feels personally responsible when he makes a hole in one.

Golf is a wonderful excuse for taking a walk and not having to take your wife or your children with you.

'Mildred, shut up,' cried the golfer at his nagging wife. 'Shut up or you'll drive me out of my mind.'

'That,' snapped Mildred, 'that wouldn't be a drive. That would be a putt.

'Why don't you play golf with Captain Fortescue any more, John?' the young wife enquired.

'Well, would you play golf with a man who talks when you're putting, fiddles his score and moves his ball out of the rough when you're not looking?'

'Certainly not!'

'Neither will the Captain.'

The Monte Carlo golf course is famed for its glorious position high in the hills behind the town – a place of lush beauty and tranquillity unless your game is off. Charlie's game was!

Not one of his shots went right. At the eighteenth hole he made a last swipe at the ball, missed completely, and tore up a metre of turf.

He then strolled disgustedly from the tee and looked down to the blue Mediterranean. Sailing boats were to be seen gliding about hundreds of metres below.

'How,' demanded Charlie, 'how can anyone be expected to shoot a decent game with those infernal ships rushing back and forth.'

A golf professional, hired by a big department store to give golf lessons, was approached by two women.

'Do you wish to learn to play golf, madam?' he asked one.

'Oh, no,' she replied, 'it's my friend who's interested in learning. I learned last Wednesday.'

'If you spend so much time at golf you won't have anything laid aside for a rainy day.'

'Oh won't I just! You should see my desk. It's just groaning with the work that I've put aside for a rainy day.'

'Can ye see your way to letting me have a golf ball, Jock?' Ian asked his old friend.

'But Ian, you said you were going to stop playing golf,' said Jock reluctantly handing over an old spare.

'By degrees, Jock. By degrees,' replied Ian pocketing the ball. 'I've stopped buying balls as a first step.'

'When can you let me have another session?' a golfer asked his professional who was a veteran of 75 years.

'Tomorrow morning,' came the reply, 'but not tomorrow afternoon. That's when I visit my father.'

'Goodness me,' exclaimed the student incredulously, 'how old is he then?'

'He's 95.'

'And he's a good player too?'

'Ah no sir – he knocks the ball about a bit – but, bless him, he'll never make a player.'

'My wife says that if I don't give up golf she'll leave me.'

'Say, that's tough, old man.'

'Yeah, I'm going to miss her.'

'Now,' said the golf pro, 'suppose you just go through the motions without driving the ball.'

'But that's precisely the difficulty I'm trying to overcome,' said his pupil.

He'd sliced his drive and watched resignedly as the ball plummeted into the woods. He followed after and found his ball – surrounded by thick undergrowth and wedged firmly between two tree roots.

He contemplated the situation for a few profoundly silent minutes then turned to his caddie and asked:

'You know what shot I'm going to take here?'

'Yes, sir,' replied the boy as he took a hip flask of malt from the bag.

'Caddiemaster, that boy isn't even eight years old.'

'Better that way, sir. He probably can't count past ten.'

The golfer arrived at the course and requested a caddie.

A young lad arrived to perform the duties and was asked by the golfer, 'Can you find lost balls?'

'Oh, yes, sir,' replied the caddie.

'Good. Then find one now and we'll make a start.'

It takes nerve to play on the Royal Nairobi course. It is bounded on three sides by a wildlife reserve where the inhabitants often enjoy grazing on greens or golfers, according to palate preferences.

The young missionary had great faith – even as he sliced his shot into a rugged area off the course. He knew he'd find his ball and did – between the forelegs of a huge and hungry lion.

As he fell quivering to his knees before the great beast the young man began to pray and to his astonishment the lion knelt also.

'Glory be to God,' exclaimed the young evangelist, 'a practising Christian lion.'

'Rowrrl,' roared the lion, 'quiet while I say grace!'

Time for a quick moral observation, the parson thought as he watched his partner's ball fly into a devilishly tricky sand trap on the fourth.

'I have observed,' he said, 'that the best golfers are not addicted to bad language.'

His partner swept a load of sand into space and, looking down at his ball still nestling between his feet, said:

'What in the bloody hell have they got to swear about?'

The new wife was trying to fathom the mysteries of the game that so occupied her spouse's time.

'What is a handicapped golfer?' she asked.

'One who plays with his boss,' came the reply.

Rich Texans are fabled for their grand style but when one oil tycoon appeared at a local British golf course followed by a servant pulling a foam-cushioned chaise-lounge, his opponents thought that this was taking style too far.

'J. R., are you going to make that poor caddie lug that couch all over the course after you?' he was asked.

'Caddie, my eye,' explained J. R. 'That's my psychiatrist.'

Isn't it great to get out on the old golf course again and lie in the sun?

The golfer completed his round in disgust and complained, 'That's dreadful! I've never played so badly before.'

'Oh,' said the caddie, 'you've played before then?'

Women are cunning golfers: they shout 'fore', hit 7, and score 3.

'My husband is very frank and outspoken,' said Molly. 'He calls a spade a spade.'

'So does mine,' nodded Ruth, 'but I couldn't repeat what he calls his golf clubs.'

Two golfers, slicing their drives into the rough, went in search of the balls. They searched for a long time without success while a dear old lady watched them with a kind and sympathetic expression.

At last, after the search had proceeded for half an hour, she addressed them sweetly.

'I hope I'm not interrupting, gentlemen,' she said, 'but would it be cheating if I told you where they are?'

'What's the matter?' Charlie asked impatiently.

Charlie and Jim were teeing off but Jim was rather a long time taking his stance.

'My wife came along with me today – she's watching me now from the clubhouse, and I want to make this next shot a good one,' Jim explained.

'Good lord,' Charlie exploded, 'you haven't got a hope of hitting her at this distance.'

He'd rejected the idea of dieting, health spas and swimming but when his doctor advised golf, the corpulent patient thought it might be worth trying. After a few weeks, however, he was back at the doctor's and asking whether he could take up some other game.

'But,' protested the doctor, 'what's wrong with golf? There's no finer game!'

'You are doubtless correct,' the patient replied, 'but my trouble is that when I put the wretched ball where I can see it I can't hit it and when I put it where I can hit it, I can't see it!'

'How many strokes d'ye have, laddie?' the Scot
asked his guest after the first hole.

'Seven.'

'I took six. Ma' hole.'

They played the second hole and once again the
Scot asked: 'How many strokes?'

'Oh no sir!' said the guest. 'It's my turn to ask.'

Saturday night and the clubhouse was crowded and noisy. The two players were drinking at the bar and discussing their game.

'Excuse me,' the barman interrupted, 'you're new members, aren't you?'

'Yes,' replied one player, 'but in all this crowd, how did you know?'

'You put your drinks down.'

While St Michael leant on his clubs, Jesus teed off. It was an awful shot. It screamed off the tee and disappeared deep in the rough. Then, suddenly a rabbit darted out onto the fairway with the ball in its mouth. Seconds later an eagle swooped down and carried the rabbit over the green. The rabbit squealed in terror and dropped the ball right into the cup. Hole in one.

St Michael turned to Jesus and said: 'Look mate, there's money on this game. Now you gonna play or fool around?'

'You think so much of your old golf game that you don't even remember when we were married.'

'Of course I do, my dear. It was the day I sank that nine-metre putt.'

And speaking of games . . .

There was this Englishman and this Scotsman who were preparing to shoot a round of golf on the Royal and Ancient Golf Club of St Andrews. The Sassenach, a bow-legged squire from the Dales, stood near the tee while the Scot made a few practice swings. Then the bow legs proved too much for the Scot and obeying a mischievous urge, he sent the ball whistling between them.

'I say, old chap,' the Englishman's tone was indignant, 'that isn't cricket.'

'No 'tis not,' grinned the highlander. 'it's good croquet, though.'

'I want you to know that this is not the game I usually play,' snapped an irate golfer to his caddie.

'I should hope not, sir. But tell me,' enquired the caddie, 'what game *do* you usually play?'

On the seventeenth of the Wentworth Club Course a very careful player was studying the green. First he got down on his hands and knees to check out the turf between his ball and the hole. Then he flicked several pieces of grass out of the way and getting up he held up a wet finger to try out the direction of the wind. Then turning to his caddie he asked:

'Was the green mowed this morning?'

'Yes, sir.'

'Right to left or left to right?'

'Right to left, sir.'

The golfer putted, missing the hole by miles. He whirled on the caddie, 'What TIME?'

'Well what do you think of my game?' the enthusiastic golfer asked his friend.

'It's OK, I guess,' replied the friend, 'but I still prefer golf.'

The club secretary was apologetic. 'I'm sorry, sir, but we have no time open on the course today.'

'Now just a minute,' the member rejoined. 'What if I told you Sean Connery and partner wanted a game. Could you find a starting time for them?'

'Yes, of course I would.'

'Well, I happen to know that he's in Scotland at the moment, so we'll take his time.'

After a three-month golfing tour in America the professional was at home in bed with his wife making up for his absence. Their romantic reunion was suddenly interrupted by a loud knocking at the door.

'Great heavens, that must be your husband!' cried the golfer, jumping out of bed and fumbling for his trousers.

'No, no. It can't be,' replied the wife. 'He's in America playing golf.'

'You surely don't want me to hole that?' the pompous amateur blustered. His ball was about thirty centimetres from the hole but his opponent, a professional answered quietly.

'No.'

The amateur picked up his ball and walked on to the next tee. He was about to take the honour when he was interrupted by his opponent.

'My honour, I think,' said the professional. 'I won the last hole, as you didn't putt out.'

'But you said you didn't want me to hole out,' spluttered the amateur.

'That's right. I didn't. And you didn't.'

Happily innocent of all golfing lore, Sam watched with interest the efforts of the man in the bunker to play his ball.

At last it rose amid a cloud of sand, hovered in the air and then dropped on the green and rolled into the hole.

'Oh my stars,' Sam chuckled, 'he'll have a tough time getting out of that one.'

To Bill's wife, golf was a total mystery. She never could understand why Bill insisted on tiring himself by walking so far every time he played.

One day she went with him to see for herself what the game was about. For six holes she tramped after him. It was on the seventh that he landed in the infamous bunker where he floundered about for some time in the sand.

She sat herself down composedly and, as the sand began to fly she happily ventured:

'There, I knew you could just as well play in one place if you made up your mind to!'

A little liquid refreshment at the nineteenth is of course all part of the game but the two Scots enthusiasts had partaken of nothing else but the national beverage throughout a long lunch break.

They returned to the links and played five holes before collecting themselves and their thoughts together.

'How do we stand, mon?' Jock asked.

'I dinna ken, Jock,' Sandy spoke very carefully. 'I'd say it was just a miracle.'

'If I died, would you remarry?' asked the wife.

'Probably would,' came the reply.

'And would you let her be your golfing partner?'

'Yes, I think so.'

'But surely you wouldn't give her my clubs?'

'Oh no. She's left-handed.'

He was a smooth operator, and at the club's annual dance he attached himself to the prettiest girl in the room and was boasting to her.

'You know, Jill, they're all afraid to play me. What do you think my handicap is?'

'I'd say your bad breath,' came the quick response.

It was a masterly addressing of the ball, a magnificent swing – but, somehow, a muddled slice shot resulted. The major's ball hit a man at full force and down he went.

The major and his partner ran up to the stricken victim who lay sprawled on the fairway. He was quite unconscious and between his legs lay the offending missile.

'Good heavens,' cried the major with considerable alarm. 'What shall I do?'

'We ought not to move him,' said his partner, 'so he becomes an immovable obstruction, and you can either play the ball as it lies or drop it two club-lengths away.'

A New Zealander holidayed in Ireland and tried out Limerick's public course, famed for its difficulty.

Driving from thick woods on the twelfth, he aimed for the fairway but as he could not see it yelled 'Fore!' and swiped. His ball struck a local player.

'Arrah, ye great mullock,' cried the Irishman, as the Kiwi emerged in pursuit of his ball.

'But I called, "Fore" and that's the signal to get out of the way.'

'Well, when oi call "Foive," that's the signal to punch your jaw! Foive!'

Overheard in the clubhouse bar:

'Giving up golf, Andy! Have you lost interest then?'

'Na, na. Lost ma ball.'

'Is Clark a good golfer?'

'Well, let me put it this way, he doesn't use a scorecard, he carries a calculator.'

A golfer is a person who can express his thoughts to a tee.

The funny thing about golf is that bankers who deal in millions can't count six strokes from tee to green.

'Did you hear about old Wilkins collapsing at the thirteenth hole?'

'Yes, Herbert gave him the kiss of life and was drunk for seven hours.'

'Can I play now, dear?' the wife asked her husband.

'Certainly dear. There's no one in the bunker,' replied her husband.

'That can't be my ball, caddie. It looks far too old.'

'It's a long time since we started, sir.'

'How does one meet new people at this club?' the recently enrolled member asked the club secretary.

'Try picking up the wrong golf ball,' the secretary replied dryly.

A noted doctor's wife asked him why he never would let her play golf with him.

'My dear,' he replied, 'there are three things a man must do alone: testify, die and putt.'

'These are terrible links, caddie. Absolutely terrible.'

'Sorry, sir, these ain't the links – we left them about forty minutes ago.'

'How can I cut down on my strokes?' asked the golfer when he cornered the professional in the shop.

'Why not take up cricket?' said the ever helpful professional.

'I have to give up golf,' Mick sadly advised the club secretary. 'I'm now so near-sighted I keep losing balls and if I play with glasses they fall off.'

'Listen,' the secretary replied, 'What about teaming up with old Bob Sullivan?'

'But he's in his 80s and can only just make it around the course.'

'Yes, yes, he's old, but he's also far-sighted and he'll see where you've hit your ball.

The next day Mick and old Bob played their first game together. Mick teed off first.

'Did you see it?' he asked Bob.

'Yes,' the old-timer answered.

'Where did it go?'

'I forget!' came the reply.

'I'll go and ask if we can go through,' said Max to Jerry.

The two golfers had been concerned for some time at the snail-like progress of two women, originally some holes ahead and now just in front of them on the ninth fairway.

Max returned after only a few paces towards the ladies.

'Jerry, this is very embarrassing, but would *you* mind going. That's my wife up ahead and she's playing with my mistress.'

Jerry returned having got no further forward than Max.

'I say,' he said, 'what a coincidence.'

Overheard on the links:

'Your trouble is that you're not addressing the ball correctly.'

'Yeah, well I've been polite to the bloody thing for long enough.'

A golfing clergyman had been beaten badly by a parishioner some thirty years his senior. He returned to the clubhouse, disappointed and a trifle depressed.

'Cheer up,' said his opponent. 'Remember, you win at the finish. You'll probably be burying me someday.'

'Yes, but even then,' said the cleric, 'it will be your hole.'

The schoolteacher was taking her first golf lesson.

'Is the word spelled "put" or "putt"?' she asked the instructor.

'"Putt" is correct,' he replied. '"Put" means to place a thing where you want it. "Putt" means merely a vain attempt to do the same thing.'

'You have got to be the worst caddie in the world!'

'Impossible, sir. That would be too much of a coincidence.'

'If I were you I'd take up golf for my health,' said the doctor after examining a patient.

'But doctor, I do play golf,' replied the man.

'In that case, I'd stop.'

'You're late teeing off, Bill.'

'Yeah, well it being Sunday I had to toss a coin to see whether I should go to church or come to golf.'

'But why so late?'

'Well, I had to toss twelve times.'

By the time a man can afford to lose a golf ball, he can't hit that far.

If looks could kill, a lot of people would die with a golf club in their hands.

'Caddie, why do you keep looking at your watch?'

'It ain't a watch, sir, it's a compass.'

For Sale: Set of golf clubs at bargain price of £100. Telephone 242424 before six o'clock. If a man answers, hang up.

Judge: 'Do you understand the nature of an oath?'
Boy:　'Do I? I'm your caddie, remember!'

'Your husband appears to go to the office much more frequently,' commented Mrs Fisher.

'Yes,' said Mrs Reid, 'his doctor said it was important he had something to take his mind off golf.'

Manchester to Melbourne, Perthshire to Palm Springs, the links on a Sunday morning get rather crowded no matter where and veterans throughout the world get irritated by delays.

Mackenzie and Brown were playing their usual weekend match on the links at Royal Sydney and were annoyed by an unusually slow twosome in front of them. One of them was seen to be mooching around on the fairway while the other was searching distractedly in the rough.

'Hey,' shouted Brown, 'why don't you help your friend find his bloody ball?'

'He's *got* his bloody ball,' came the reply. 'It's his bloody club he's looking for.

A golfer has one advantage over a fisherman. He doesn't have to produce anything to prove his story.

After a series of disastrous holes, the strictly amateur golfer in an effort to smother his rage laughed hollowly and said to his caddie:

'This golf is a funny game.'

'It's not supposed to be,' said the boy gravely.

The lady golfer was a determined, if not very proficient player. At each swipe she made at the ball earth flew in all directions.

'Gracious me,' she exclaimed red-faced to her caddie, 'the worms will think there's an earthquake.'

'I don't know,' replied the caddie, 'the worms round here are very clever. I'll bet most of them are hiding underneath the ball for safety.'

At a Surrey golf club two sedate matrons were playing when a flasher rushed out of the bushes clad in nothing at all.

'Sir,' asked the older of the two players severely, 'are you a member?'

'My game's really improving, dear.'
   'How's that, Mavis?'
   'I hit a ball in one today.'

'Lost your job as a caddie?' asked the father.
   'Yes,' replied his son. 'I could do the job all right, but I couldn't learn not to laugh.'

'Your ball hit me!'
  'Not mine, it was my husband's.'
  'What are you going to do about it?'
  'Want to hit him back?'

'**B**ill, I'm giving up, I've swung at that wee ball ten times and missed it every time.'

'Keep trying dear. You've got it looking a bit worried.'

The two Irishmen were strolling along the fairway when they heard the warning shout 'Fore!' and a golf ball whizzed past them. Immediately the two men threw themselves to the ground and one gasped, 'Don't move! There must be three more to come!'

The argumentative drunk in the club bar had been looking for a fight all afternoon since losing his game. Finally he threw a punch at the player on the nearest bar stool. He ducked and the drunk, losing balance, fell off his stool and onto the floor. By the time he'd disentangled himself from bar stools and dusted himself off, his opponent had left.

'D'ya see that, barman?' he complained. 'Not much of a fighter was he?'

'Not much of a driver either, sir. He's just driven over your clubs,' said the barman gazing out the window.

Golfer: 'Notice any improvement today, Jimmy?'
Caddie: 'Yes, ma'am. You've had your hair done.'

A newcomer had come to learn the great game.

'And how does one play this game?' he asked his caddie.

'Basically sir, all you have to do is hit the ball in the direction of that flag over there.'

'Right ho,' and the novice teed off. It was a magnificent drive that took his ball right down the centre of the fairway. And, unbelievably, it landed on the green only a few centimetres from the hole.

'What do I do now?' asked the novice.

'Just hit the ball into the hole sir,' said the caddie in some excitement. 'That's the whole idea of the game.'

'*Now* you tell me!'

The old golfer paced anxiously up and down outside the emergency room of the East Lothian Hospital near Muirfield Golf Course. Inside the doctors were operating to remove a golf ball accidentally driven down a player's throat.

The sister-in-charge noticed the old golfer and went to reassure him.

'It won't be long now,' she said. 'You're a relative?'

'No, no, lassie. It's my ball.'

'I've just killed my wife,' cried the hysterical golfer rushing into the clubhouse. 'I didn't see her. She was behind me you see,' he sobbed, 'and I started my back swing and clipper her right between the eyes. She must have died on the instant.'

'What club were you using?' asked a concerned bystander.

'Oh, the No. 2 iron.'

'Oh, oh,' murmured the other, 'that's the club that always gets me into trouble too.'

The sky above was blue and cloudless. If the judge had been a lawmaker instead of a law interpreter he knew he would be making laws forbidding court sessions on such glorious days.

'Well,' he mused, dragging his eyes back to the court, 'I guess there's no way out. I might just as well tune back in on the case.'

'And in addition to that, Your Honour,' the barrister for the defence was droning, 'my client claims she was beaten into insensibility by a golf club in the hand of her husband.

'How many strokes?' murmured the judge absently.

Nothing counts in a golf game like your opponent.

In the locker room the two golfers prepared to go out and do battle on the course and as John lifted his bag he said, 'Now just remember, Fred, that casual water means a temporary pool caused by rain, hail or snow; not going behind a tree for a pee.'

'Good lord, Binky,' the old admiral roared to his friend as he came into the clubhouse looking anything but pleased. 'I've just been playing with a chappie from the Treasury. One of those civil service wallahs.'

'Good oh, Bunny,' replied the other old regular absently. 'Bring him in for a drink.'

'Can't,' replied the old sea dog. 'Playing the sixteenth someone shouted "fore" and the blighter sat down to wait for a cup of tea. I've come in and left him sitting there.'

The four friends were out enjoying a brisk game. As the men moved on to the green a funeral procession moved slowly past along the nearby road and one of the foursome removed his cap and stood with his head solemnly bowed.

One of his friends noticed his action and was abashed.

'My gosh, Jim. You remind us all of our manners. It's not often though that one sees such a genuine gesture of respect for the dead.'

'Oh, it's the least I could do,' replied the man. 'You know in six more days we would have been married twenty-five years.'

The golfer and his caddie enjoyed a good argument, especially about what clubs to use. The caddie usually won but this day, faced with a long short hole, the golfer decided that a 3-iron would be best.

'Take a spoon,' growled the caddie.

But the golfer stuck to his choice and the caddie watched gloomily as the ball sailed over the fairway and rolled politely into the hole.

'You see,' grinned the triumphant golfer.

'You would have done still better with your spoon,' came the dogged reply.

At the Glenelg seaside course in South Australia a novice managed a mighty drive off the first tee. It hit, and bounced off in rapid succession, a rock outcrop, a fisherman, a tree trunk, the handle of a golf cart, a player on the second tee and finally it dropped onto the green about ten centimetres from the hole.

'Well,' the played exclaimed, 'if only I'd hit the bloody ball a bit harder!'

An old tramp wandered leisurely up to the green of the eighteenth where he sat himself down among his many coats. He dug among the variety of old bags he was carrying and brought forth with great pomp a handful of dried twigs.

Members watched as he got his campfire going. The tranquillity of the scene was shattered when a man dashed from the clubhouse and ordered the tramp off the course.

'Well, just who do you think you are,' asked the tramp.

'I'm the club secretary,' shouted the man.

'Well, listen sonny,' the tramp retorted. 'Let me give you some advice. That's hardly the way to get new members.'

He had just come in from a long afternoon at golf. His wife kissed him and kissed their son who came in a few seconds later.

'Where's he been?' the husband asked.

'He's been caddying for you all afternoon,' the wife replied.

'No wonder that kid looked so familiar!'

'Really, I can't play golf,' said the blonde. 'I don't even know how to hold the caddie.'

'I find golf is very educational,' said the first wife.

'How is that?' asked the second wife.

'Well, every time my husband turns the television on to watch golf I go into another room and read a book,' replied the first wife.

'I say greenkeeper, I dropped my bottle of Scotch
out of the bag somewhere on the seventh.
Anything handed in at lost-and-found?'

'Only the golfer who played after you, sir.'

Misjudging its depth, Ron went wading into the lake to retrieve his badly sliced ball. Very quickly he was floundering out of his depth and, as his tweed plus-fours became waterlogged, found himself in real trouble.

'Help, I'm drowning!' he shouted to his partner.

'Don't worry,' came the reply. 'You won't drown. You'll never keep your head down long enough.'

The party games were a triumph and now the
marble tournament was in full swing. Then six-year-
old Simon missed an easy shot and let fly with a
potent expletive.

'Simon,' his mother remonstrated in
embarrassment from the sidelines, 'what do little
boys who swear when they are playing marbles
turn into?'

'Golfers,' Simon replied.

An Australian touring round Britain was playing on a small course in Devonshire. He was on the first green and about to putt when he was suddenly beset by a flock of seagulls.

'Piss off, will ya',' he cried, thrashing at the birds.

A sweet little old lady who was sitting knitting near the green came over to speak to him.

'Excuse me,' she said. 'There's no need to speak to the little birdies like that. All you need to say is "Shoo shoo little birdies!" Then they'll piss off.'

As the two players approached the ninth tee they noticed what appeared to be a small picnic party assembled right on the spot.

'Here, what are you doing with our tee?' one called out.

'Garn, it ain't yours,' came the retort. 'We brought it wiv us all the way from Bermondsey.'

Sam and Janet were beginning a game of golf. Janet stepped to the tee, and her first drive gave her a hole in one. Sam stepped up to the tee and said, 'OK, now I'll take my practice swing, and then we'll start the game.'

Eric, the club's worst golfer, was addressing his ball. Feet apart, just so, a few practice wiffles with the driver, just so, then swing. He missed. The procedure was repeated and then repeated again. On the fourth swing however he did manage to connect with his ball and drove it five metres down the fairway. Looking up in exasperation he was a stranger who had stopped to watch him.

'Look here!' Eric shouted angrily. 'Only golfers are allowed on this course!'

The stranger nodded, 'I know it, mister,' he replied. 'But I won't say anything if you won't either!'

Two long-time enthusiasts were discussing their scores over a beer in the clubhouse.

'I can't understand it one cried disgustedly. 'I've been playing golf for fifteen years now and I get worse every year. Do you know, last year I played worse than the year before. And the year before that, same thing.

'That's depressing,' commiserated the other. 'How're you doing this year?'

'Put it this way,' said the first, nursing his beer unhappily. 'I am already playing next year's game.'

'Golf is a good walk spoiled.'

Mark Twain

'What did your husband say when you missed that short putt on the fifteenth?' enquired Winnie.

'Shall I leave out the swear words?' asked Betty.

'Yes.'

'Nothing,' sighed Betty

That he was a wealthy American tourist was obvious. On his arrival at a small Irish hotel the tiny reception area became full in an instant. Not only were there suitcases but also golf clubs, golf shoes, golf umbrellas and several boxes of balls.

'Surely now, sor,' cried the manager eyeing the baggage with alarm, 'there must be some mistake. We've no golf course you see and you'll be finding there's not one within miles of the place.'

'Well now, that's no problem,' drawled the tourist. 'I'm having one sent over with my heavy baggage.'

Explorer: 'There we were surrounded. Fierce
savages everywhere you looked.
They uttered awful cries and beat
their clubs on the ground . . .'

Weary listener: 'Golfers, probably.'

Did you hear about the player who spent so much time in the bunker he got mail addressed to Hitler?

One golfer spent so much time in the sand traps he was known to the other club members as Lawrence of Arabia.

Talk about fantastic golf teachers. He was the best and one day this woman came to him and said that she had developed a terrific slice.

Day and night he worked with her for five months. Now she's the biggest hooker in town.

'That's good for one long drive and a putt,' said the cocky golfer as he teed his ball and looked down the fairway to the green. He swung mightily and hit his ball which landed about a metre from the tee.

His caddie handed him a club and remarked: 'And now for one hell of a putt.'

The caddie had an embarrassing vocabulary and reputation. He'd been assigned to caddie for the local Anglican bishop and warned by the caddiemaster to say nothing unless spoken to.

Things went well for a couple of holes. Then on the third the bishop's stroke was not quite clean.

'Where did that sod go, caddie?' asked the churchman looking to replace a divot he'd shifted.

'Into the bloody bunker,' retorted the caddie who'd watched the ball, 'and don't forget you started it.'

HELP YOURS[ELF]
ALL
EQUIPME[NT]
FREE

Good
heavens.

Having led a dissolute life, the new arrival was not too surprised to find himself in hell. He was however surprised to find it was a golf course complete with the usual professional's shop. His delight was complete when he read the shop's notice: Help yourself – everything free.

'Well, this is going to be tough,' he leered as he chose a bag containing perfectly matched clubs. He ambled to the first tee where he felt in the ball pocket. It was empty.

He was about to return to the shop when he noticed a grinning figure in red.

'Don't mind me,' the grin grew wider, 'and don't bother going back for balls. There aren't any. That's the hell of it!'

Friendly golfer (to player searching for lost ball):
'What sort of a ball was it?'
Caddie:
'A brand new one – never been properly hit yet!'

'**C**addie, I suppose you've seen worse golfers in your thirty years at the club . . . caddie, I said I suppose you've seen worse golfers,' panted the struggling player.

'I heard you the first time, sir, I'm just trying to remember,' answered the caddie.

Mark Twain accompanied a friend and watched while the friend played golf. Repeatedly during the game more turf was hit than golf balls and dirt went flying after every stroke.

Finally the friend turned to Twain and enquired how he liked the links

'Best I ever tasted,' came the swift reply.

The tall highlander walked into the shop at Pitlochry Golf Club and stood ramrod straight as he pulled a badly nicked ball from his sporran.

'What can you do?' he asked the manager.

'Well,' said the manager in complete understanding, 'we can vulcanise it for five pence or re-cover it for ten.'

'I'll let ye know t'morra,' said the customer.

The next day he was back, holding out the ball. 'Tha' Regiment,' he said, 'votes ta' vulcanise.'

Bob and Ken had played golf for over twenty years and, for over twenty years, Bob had lost each game. Bob decided to get the greatest partner to help him win. So he found this giant Irish wharf labourer and got him on side.

They were out on the first tee with the hole some 400 metres off and the giant hit a tremendous drive which landed the ball on the green.

'I can't beat that,' Ken moaned. 'He'll probably go two on every hole. Here's the money. Incidentally, though, how does he putt?'

Bob carefully pocketed his win. 'Same way he drives,' he replied.

He was not what you'd call an expert player. Time after time he would hit his brand new balls where they couldn't be retrieved or even found. Balls went into the lake, out of bounds, across the highway, into the woods, and on one memorable occasion into a stormwater drain that was being built near the course.

It was after that shot that one of the members of his foursome suggested, 'Why don't you use an old ball on those difficult shots?'

'An old ball?' the benighted player cried. 'The way I play, it's obvious I've never had an old ball!'

'Let me inform you, young man,' said the slow elderly golfer, 'I was playing this game before you were born.'

'That's all very well, but I'd be obliged if you'd try to finish it before I die.'

On one occasion Errol Flynn and W. C. Fields were playing golf when Fields dislocated his knee. Flynn helped him back to the clubhouse where the professional offered to push the knee back in.

'But it will be quite painful,' he warned.

'Proceed, my good man,' said Fields, taking a long swig from his indispensable hip flask. 'Pain means nothing to me.'

The pro took a firm grip on the knee and pushed hard. Fields let out a howl of pain.

'Easy, Mr Fields,' said the pro. 'My wife's just had a baby and she didn't make half that fuss.'

'Yes, but they weren't trying to push it back in,' retorted Fields.

On another occasion W. C. Fields was asked if he believed in clubs for women.

'Yes,' he answered, 'if every other form of persuasion fails.'

One day on the sixth, W. C. Fields played a terrible shot, hooking the ball deep into the trees.

'That's the same shot as you played yesterday,' rebuked his caddie.

'Not at all, my withered little friend, not at all. Yesterday I played that stroke after drinking a bottle of gin, today I played it after drinking a bottle of vodka,' replied Fields.

And talk about hazards . . .

At New Zealand's Rotorua Club they include bubbling mud pools, quicksand and steaming geysers and the water hazards are hot and fast flowing.

A visiting American player on the twelfth came across a quicksand bog. Extending from it was a hand gesticulating wildly.

'My, oh my,' said the Yank, 'is he signalling for his wedge?'

A group of golfers were putting on the green when suddenly a ball dropped in their midst. One of the party winked at the others and shoved the ball into the hole with his foot.

Seconds later a very fat player puffed on to the green and asked: 'Seen my ball?'

'Yeah, it went in the hole,' the joker answered with straight-faced alacrity.

The fat one looked at him unbelievingly, walked to the hole, looked in and picked up his ball. His astonishment was plain to see. Then he turned, ran down the fairway and the group heard him shout:

'Hey, Sam, I got an eleven.'